The Fame Factors

Modern Day Business Communications

To Help Close the Deal

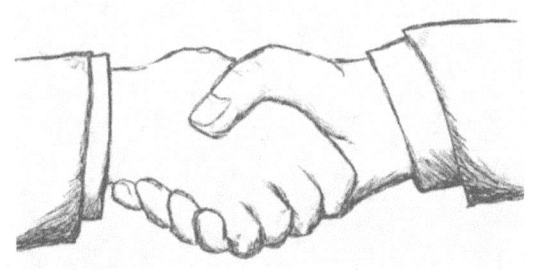

PATRICIA OGILVIE

Copyright © 2018 by PEL
All rights reserved.
No part of this publication may be
reproduced or transmitted in any form or by any means,
electronic, or mechanical, including photocopying,
recording, or by any information storage and retrieval
system, without permission in writing from the publisher.
Published by ProRisk Press, Box 253,
Alberta Beach, Alberta, Canada T0E 0A0
Website: https:/auntisays.com

Revised, Updated & Modernized 2nd Edition

"ProRisk Press"

ISBN: 9781729350720

DEDICATION

To my Circle of People who Appreciate and Include me.

Table of Contents

ACKNOWLEDGMENTS vii

1. From Then to Now 1

2. What's Fame? 6

3. Your Right to be Famous 12

4. L—Live Your Dreams 15

5. A—Address Your Audience 40

6. U—Unique About You? 48

7. G—Get Proof and Give Proof 53

8. H—Headline: Your Best Friend 59

9. T—Tighten the Content 64

10. E—Engage Their Emotions 70

11. R—Results: Your Selling Solution 75

Concluding Remarks 79

ABOUT THE AUTHOR 88

PATRICIA OGILVIE

ACKNOWLEDGMENTS

Creating Business Recognition: Fame that is, is conveniently outlined in this acronym:
L.A.U.G.H.T.E.R.

This is one of the easiest ways of remembering the steps in this process. And I want your experience to be the easiest possible.

But here's the thing. You must first decide that you really want to get famous. Are you open to receiving more profits, attention, and ultimately, recognition? Next you must accept that the journey is actually a process. And most important, decide to have fun!

This process is what my brother coined "ass backwards". When you bring your own personal recognition to the fame table, then and only then will your customer bring hers or his? This is another important factor to consider.

And then there's this factor. That fame and success are not usually instant – they take some time to create.

Success is not just a process, it takes time. Are you willing to accept these claims? If you're nodding your head yes, then let's get going.

Each letter signifies an important step to creating your Direct Response marketing copy to its final result. In this book you are encouraged to write a sales letter about something you wish to promote.

Your result is your best-written version of 'what' your company offers: and remember, it's not necessarily the product or service!

Let me explain. It's not your book, or your presentations, or your consult, or product or service. It's what the customer will gain from having experienced your product or service. So, what are you really selling?

Are your customers laughing out loud with gratitude they found you?

Are you laughing all the way to the bank?

These eight practical modules lead you step-by-step to your desired **Result: A Selling Solution.** This selling solution will be transformed into your website pages, a sales letter, a brochure, an advertisement, or a powerful news release to promote your business. The best part? You can do this in as little time as **One Afternoon!**

L. Live Your Dream!

A. Address Your Audience.

U. Unique About You?

G. Get Proof – Give Proof

H. Headlines - Your Best Friend!

T. Tighten The Copy!

E. Engage Their Emotions

R. Results: Your Famous Selling Solution

The reason you want to write the most persuasive and compelling document is because you want to convince others to buy from you.

Why L.A.U.G.H.T.E.R? It begets fun. Fun gets transferred to your career, your business and your customer. No other reason.

I'll probably repeat myself throughout this book: your energy is a critical fame factor. How you feel when you write your marketing material gets transferred. Attitude is a fame factor.

Ready To Sell? Your main goal is to sell. It is proved over and over by direct mail and web marketing professionals that one of the best models that attracts your customer is a simple sales letter. We'll work on one together in the following chapters.

Thank you brother, sister, and friends who believe in me. This is for you, for your courage and dedication to making life brilliant.

1. FROM THEN TO NOW

The heart of this book began over 10 years ago. In fact, I wrote the 1st Edition in 2006. And as I rewrote some of the chapters, added new content about mobile culture, websites, social media and changes in how people consume and communicate, I noticed nothing had changed from a direct response marketing aspect!

The tools are just as powerful today as they were a decade ago.

What does that tell you? That asking for what you want is still the real reason to be in business!

Business supports the economy; it strengthens confidence and hopefully, increases profits so you enjoy your life.

The only difference now from then is you have a multitude of other avenues **for sharing your message.**

Back then I was speaking to groups of entrepreneurs about how to write dynamic and compelling sales copy for their products and services. As I spoke about Direct Response Copywriting - writing that asks for the order right in the copy itself - they asked some revealing questions.

These were hard questions that surprisingly weren't about copy. They were questions that their customers were asking them. You'll read those questions in a moment, but first:

Your Customer Determines Your Business Approach

That's what this book is about – creating direct response advertising in all sorts of marketing venues that answers your customers' questions and solidifies their commitment to your business. And your business gets the recognition it deserves.

Just to clarify, direct response advertising is not agency advertising – direct response ad writing is the kind of advertising that makes people open their checkbooks and buy - not next week, not tomorrow, but right now.

My audiences wanted a piece of that.

They Also Wanted to Get Famous!

The aspect of fame came up at the same time because they realized that this marketing strategy could actually get the customer excited about any product or service and buy it right then and there.

They saw the potential of this type of selling – direct-response selling – could be done through radio, print, the Internet and TV ads. In fact, they saw the potential to be unique and distinct in their customers' eyes. They saw real cash flow. They saw fame. However, they also feared fame!

They also saw the potential of actually being able to relate to their customer – offering her a book that would make her more attractive to the opposite sex... a process that will help him get rich ... or be healthier ... or shed unwanted pounds. No matter what the customer wanted, this style of copy could touch the customer's heart. And yet, there was fear surrounding writing quality marketing copy.

This Is One of The Most Important Factors Contributing to Your Fame.

After studying the results of other very powerful, very profitable and very famous entrepreneurs who used direct response to sell projects and services, I discovered how they created, developed and maintained customer commitment. I learned what they did to ensure their business was recognized.

They built respect and admiration. Ready to see just how they did it?

Here's what I discovered:

There's Only This Way to Become Famous in Business:

Give her what *she* desires – fill her core emotional needs – she becomes loyal - you become famous.

To experience effortless fame is to experience powerful customer relations with your customer.

When you answer your customer's deep-rooted concerns, then and only then, will you become famous.

It is absolutely essential to make certain that you put yourself inside the mind of your customer. Think as she thinks; feel what she feels. Become your customer.

The more you feel equality with your customer, the more you feel like she does, the more she will experience your best offering. Equality - that's another critical factor for creating recognition.

Most importantly, vercome any fears about your own success and growth.

Carefully make sure that every ad you write or pay for answers these five essential questions your customer absolutely demands attention to (and they don't even consciously know it):

Five Customer Questions

Just imagine for a moment your customer is sitting in front of you. She asks these questions:

"Does your ad make me crave this kind of product by touching my emotional needs?"

"Does your ad explain all the reasons why your brand is the only one I should consider?"

"Does your ad make me feel it's urgent that I buy your product now – or at least soon?"

"Do I have everything I need to know to make the purchase?"

"Does your company just want my money, or do you truly want to help me?"

Fame Is Possible

You may wonder as you read through this book, if this process can be proven to create fame. Let me answer this way. I can offer the precise formula for creating fame. And if you follow this process exactly as this book tells you, you will surely become famous.

However, if for whatever reason you leave out a step, particularly engaging your certainty that you do deserve fame, you will most likely fail to achieve your desired target.

I'll talk more about this certainty (uncertainty) in detail in an upcoming Chapter. For now, I would encourage you to read again your customer's questions. Let's pay particular attention to the fifth.

"Does your company just want my money, or do you truly want to help me?"

You Have a Beautiful Mind

In 1948, Professor John Nash challenged and proved Adam Smith incorrect in his organizational strategy, a strategy, businesses used for decades: if each one did what was best for himself, everybody would win. Instead, Nash scientifically demonstrated: if each one did what was best for himself *AND* consideration for the rest of the group at the same time, then everybody would win. He received the Nobel Prize for this concept in 1994. The concept is none other than win-win. A movie honored this great thinker. In 2001, the Australian actor Russell Crowe portrayed Nash in the movie, *A Beautiful Mind*.

Win-win is becoming the invaluable concept it deserves to be.

Here then lies the third factor you must consider in order to achieve fame. Regard others as if they are also honorable.

"Dependent people need others to get what they want. Independent people can get what they want through their own efforts. Interdependent people combine their own efforts with the efforts of others to achieve their greatest success." —Stephen Covey

2. WHAT'S FAME?

In the coming Chapters, I will reveal my top strategies for devising, researching and writing your direct response ads that could make you famous.

Your copy could be in the form of a web home page or the *sales letter* you need to jump-start your business and make the profits you say you want. Ultimately, you want to be recognized for the brilliance that you are. You want to get famous.

Defining Fame

What does fame mean to you? Quite simply, when someone else recognizes you, your business, your product or service, you are automatically famous. Yep, that's it. It's that easy.

And what else does fame mean? It is glory, distinction and honor.

Is your business fulfilling these famous attributes?

Well it's time to do something about it if you're not yet where you desire. And the following tips and strategies give you a practical approach to creating marketing material that enhance your business.

You Are the Expert in Your Field

Whatever your line of business, when potential clients see your unique sales presentation, they will view you as a serious player—someone who obviously knows his or her field inside out. I'm sure I don't need to belabor the many advantages this will bring you in selling your products and services.

You will discover how to effectively create your own sales literature following these simple step-by-step modules either for a precise 10-word ad, a 30-page magalog, or the most powerful marketing tool—your website.

The Energy of Clarity

Your product, service or you (your business) **transfers energy** to your customer. Your customer **receives your energy** even if it's from social media, website, a letter, a news release, an ad or you personally.

Without clarity you could be transferring mixed messages and maybe even negative energy which the customer unconsciously picks up. They wonder why they don't relate to you. They give it a moment of thought, then they're gone.

Or you may be sending confusing energy—you know the kind; you're not exactly sure what you have to offer and how it will benefit your customer.

Clarity is Key

You know **where you currently stand**.
You know **what your goals are**.
You know **where you are going** with your business.
You know **how to motivate yourself**.
You know **who to get help from**.
You know **when to handle obstacles** as they come up

regarding all aspects of your business.

Now that's powerful. Right now, having this type of information ready, you have the passion to offer your customer her desired solutions.

If you don't—if you're not clear about what you want out of your business, refocus on the six bullets above. Know them first. This step is important in achieving fame. Please don't miss it.

Frankly, My Dear, Thanks for Giving a Damn!

That would be music to your ears, wouldn't it? Hearing your clients say, thanks for giving a damn! And how often have you felt appreciated? All the time? Most of the time? Or seldom?

BUT…The Trick Is: It's Not About You!

Let me explain. I learned that giving my customer what she wanted was the only way to get what I wanted—and I had to be honest about what I wanted: appreciation, money and fame.

Here's what happened.

As a former systems analyst I could relate to the delicate and detailed analysis required to create projects, especially computer systems. Everyone had to be considered; each department and each employee's needs had to be included into the overall project plan.

However, sometimes impatience and short cuts take precedence. And unfortunately, the energy of impatience spread its slimy tendrils throughout this particular project I was working on.

To meet a deadline, assumptions were made about what not just one, but two departments required from the developing database. The assumptions were wrong. After eight months of development, and after over eight hundred thousand dollars, the project had to be completely redone—

at the developer's expense (the company I worked for).

Now, here's the huge lesson and mistake I am letting you know about—the ongoing contract was not extended. A new systems development firm took over.

The client hated us. We oozed impatience and our results proved it. Our client never did give us what we wanted. Truth is, we forgot to give a damn about what they wanted! We were 100% focused on what was in it for us.

I don't know what the other members of our team wanted. I can only admit that at the time, I wanted a quick turnaround.

Now if you think this mindset doesn't transfer over to the customer, if you think a client doesn't pick up on insensitivity or lethargy, you may as well stop reading.

I'm being totally sincere now when I say this, "You must understand this principle in order to succeed." Frankly, the entrepreneurs I researched for this book earned fame by giving their customers what they wanted. They understood throughout their marketing campaigns that attitude towards their revered customer was tantamount to success.

Your Customer Wants Very Badly to Feel Very Good

Ask yourself: in your own business, do your customers stay for the duration?

Does your audience anticipate your support and pleasure at offering them what they want?

Are they getting value?

Do they feel like you give a damn about them?

I'm referring to the performance your web site or your sales letter does on your business behalf. How about your business card or brochure? Is it pulling in your customer? Is it giving them a powerful benefit-based, emotionally driven "craving," to do business with you? Do they get the message you care about their needs?

Because It's All About Them!

If your marketing and business mission is to deluge them with reams of information about *you*, you've made no impact! That's right, no impact! No value! Your customer wants to know what's in it for *them*.

Bottom line: there's only one way to hear those sweet words from your customer base, "Thanks!" and that's to give them what they want—a powerful, benefit-based, emotionally-driven promise that you care. Because, being and staying in business is *Not About You!* *[Remind yourself of Facebook 2018]*

How to Collect and Keep the Dime!

It's your job to ensure your customer receives a greater value. I learned a valuable sales lesson—my customer truly wants to feel part of my business, not just a commodity outside looking in. And as long as I was willing to be vulnerable, so were they. And the key is, know your customer. Do your research. What do they really want from you?

You Are an "Idea Generator" and "Problem Solver"

In order to achieve fame, you must conclude that you are not just a product or service provider. You are now a problem solver and an idea generator—people look up to you for help.

Famous Entrepreneurs Transfer the Right Energy

Remember, successful entrepreneurs don't hire experts to run their businesses. First, they figure it out for themselves.

When it comes to making your product or project visible to your customer base, rely on nobody but yourself to make sure it gets done right. It may be stressful and time-consuming to do a lot of extra work by yourself, but it will pay in the long run. You will understand the project in an intimate, extremely valuable way. Eventually you will pass the project on to your employees.

However, you first make sure you have the right energy. Then **you** transfer the energy. Get exited first, then transfer that energy. It's miraculous to watch.

Attitude Is Just as Thick on Paper or Computer Screen

You've probably heard this: the energy was so thick, you could cut it with a knife.

That's how powerful your energy emanates. And you know what else? It shows up in words on paper. It shows up thicker on social media and on your website. So that means, if not you, whoever you hire to write your advertising copy is putting his or her energy into "your" message.

You're probably wondering why all this is so important. Well, I've been writing copy for websites and various advertising projects since 2001 and have helped thousands of people get online, visible and mobile.

Over the years, technology has advanced and of the billions of people who search websites and social media, most do so from smart phones and pads—the phone book and written advertisement are basically the way of the do-do! Extinct. (not totally, but less than we can even imagine)

3. YOUR RIGHT TO BE FAMOUS

Imagine how good you feel knowing your reputation is solid and honorable!

Imagine how good your customer feels doing business with you!

Imagine ... FAME.

Fame is not so fickle that she can't be snagged. What you will discover is that there is nothing wrong in wanting to get famous. The desire for fame complements the desire for riches. And that desire is merely a deep longing for a richer, fuller and more abundant life.

This book guides you into your real journey into a self-awareness of just how much you and your business are respected by your customers and clients.

This journey will take you into a level of self-respect you may not have yet experienced. So, please, enjoy the ride and get ready to become famous.

"You can only help them find it within themselves"--Galileo Galilee

Before you begin achieving L.A.U.G.H.T.E.R., remind yourself just how worthwhile and creative you are. That's how you build fame and respect.

The Power Is In Your Belief

The power of thought is a much-written-about subject. So why hasn't the regular person applied this to a regular work situation?

Every thought about a colleague, work environment, and your customer is like a seed that when allowed to grow in the mind, takes root, produces its own and sooner or later becomes results.

If positive, your outer circumstance shapes itself to reflect your thinking.

If negative, your results are reshaped accordingly.

Good thoughts bear good fruit; bad thoughts bad fruit. Sound reasonable? Actually, it's not such a well-known concept.

The little-known powerful principle states that the *belief* underlying the thought is what triggers the ongoing thinking. The belief can be changed if it is not supporting you in achieving what you want.

The Thinking Stuff Of Fame

Many thoughts come from your unconscious. If they surface into your brain and feel good - go for it! If they surface and feel bad, stop! Stop thinking and release that mindset. It is harmful to you! Rethink to a vision of yourself successful and respected. It truly is that simple. Let me ask you this: Do you believe it?

Only you can decide whether to believe in this process.

Tell One Story Every Day

One of the most effective methods used to help create a new belief: "I deserve to be famous. I am famous!" is through the process of story-telling.

Children in their formative years cannot grasp facts. Their belief systems are developed through story telling.

Stories become the practical way of becoming aware of the inner chatter in your mind. Hearing what you really tell yourself can be interesting. Surprising. Even astounding. Have you ever stood, looking glassy eyed and wondering, scratching your head and muttering under your breath, "How the hell did I get into this mess?"

Most Messes Can Be Straightened

You have a choice as an intelligent, informed reader.

You can test some strategies to help yourself experience your role with ease and joy or you can do what over 51% of the world population does, turn your back on your dreams, visions and legacies and kick them under the bed with the dust balls for another few years.

You can live up to your potential remembering you are always respected, or you can give up your potential by blaming others for where you are and who you are.

It's always choice.

Most of the self-help advocates out there tell you to turn your back on fears and negativity. But I'm here to tell you that you need to face them, honor them, acknowledge them and that's when they lose power!

"The longer we dwell on our misfortunes, the greater is their power to harm us." -- Voltaire

4. L—LIVE YOUR DREAMS

It is one thing to motivate your customers; it is another to motivate yourself.

Successful entrepreneurs use this well-established, step-by-step formula for all forms of sales copy including direct mail, e-mail, and Internet promotions. However, they first strengthen their circumstances by ensuring their emotions are congruent to communicating what they offer.

They develop the energy of passion and **excitement** before sitting down to write ads. Then and only then they are guaranteed that their writing has clear intention and a desire to persuade.

- Get attention. Write an effective headline or teaser that grabs your reader and holds on for days!

- Identify the problem or need. Orient your prospect and put her in a receptive mood for what is to come. In other words, expand a bit more on the main benefit your headline shouts to them.

- Position your product as the solution. Use a quick transition to switch your reader from thinking about the problem to thinking about the perfect solution you offer.

- Prove your product is the best solution. Provide a list of satisfied clients, testimonials, case histories, or a description of your product's features and benefits.

- Repeat the main benefit, include the price and ask for the order. Present a clear offer and ask your reader to accept it.

- Tell your reader exactly how to get the product or service. And foremost, don't assume the reader will know anything more than what you've included in the copy.

Sound simple enough. In fact, it is. However, what gets in the way of even the simplest outline is the frame of mind it is written in. Before we get to the specifics of the writing, I believe this aspect needs to be addressed in more detail.

The key to more L.A.U.G.H.T.E.R. and increased profits in your business is to believe it is possible.

SCIENCE 101 – Behavior Changes Attitude!

Believing precedes action!

This concept can be confusing so bear with me. The simplicity of this statement proves that attitude can change behavior. The more common belief is that behavior changes attitude.

Put differently, being famous doesn't depend as much on whether you are a positive person or a negative one. It does, however, depend on the specific actions and attitude you decide to take, or fail to take, to build it. Let me ask you this. Do you act as if you are already famous?

"To serve is beautiful, but only if it is done with joy and a whole heart."-- Pearl S. Buck

The bottom line is fame goes hand in hand with building relationships. What's more, most of the time, we are so busy looking for people with whom to build a relationship with that we forget that they are right in front of us all the time.

Getting fame is not always a result of doing the right things or of being in the right place at the right time. Fame comes from being the right person/business. **People attract to their lives not what they want but what they are! I'll ask you again, "Do you believe you deserve the gifts in front of you and do you act as if you are famous?"**

If not, you've a long and difficult road ahead.

So, let's try something different. As of now, believe you are already famous, and your customer wants a part of that.

Outer experience is a reflection of inner beliefs about personal self-worth. And here's the best part! As you notch up your self-worth, you automatically attract better and better things into your life! You automatically invite respect! You automatically get fame!

Expect Fame…

Decide to be certain you will attract your dream of being so famous; you get repeat customers and referrals.

One principle you need to understand above all others is based on the Law of Attraction - like attracts like. Add that to a piece of knowledge from quantum physics that says when a thought is held for 16 seconds, it attracts more similar matter. So, if you spend more than 16 seconds complaining or thinking about a problem, you will attract more and more similar thoughts and circumstances.

You may have on occasion been guilty of thinking about something over and over, blowing it out of proportion, and notice that the situation worsens the more you focus on it. What if you spent 16 seconds of focused energy on thinking and speaking about positives so *more like* thoughts are brought in and more inspired actions can come?

Lessons from Grade Seven

Remember this experiment from Grade Seven science? Take three tuning forks of which two were of a similar pitch and one different. Ping one and see which of the other sings. The one with the same frequency will vibrate. The one with a different frequency won't because only like frequencies attract.

Your thoughts and feelings are the same when it comes to frequencies and they are also magnetic. Those relationships with like beliefs, thoughts and interests, attract each other. If someone is different, the likelihood of that person participating with you is negligible.

More Lessons from Grade Seven

Try this simple exercise. Take two wire coat hangers and make two "L" shapes. Make the shorter length of the "L" about 6". The longer will be about a foot. Hold both hangers by the 6" part pointing just like pistol-toting Pete would. Keep them loose. Think of something ugly from your past. The wires separate quickly. Think of something happy. The wires come together. Play and see how magnetic you really are.

The Teenager's Malady

Remember junior high school? Remember how you thought of yourself in those pubescent years? If you experienced pain, it's more than likely you didn't feel good about yourself. Heck it was difficult going through all those hormonal phases.

Most teenagers probably went through this. Hopefully you're not still stuck there.

This is an example of how your thoughts are like magnets. Send ugly thoughts to your colleagues. Do you think they don't feel it? They most certainly do. Have you felt someone's presence as being comfortable to be in? How about someone you didn't feel good with? Are you one of those who transmit uncomfortable or comfortable vibrations out? Because, you will get back what you predominantly send out.

Similarly, the messages you send yourself also affect you. If you think of yourself as fat, ugly, stupid, rotten, unlovable or plain old rodent type, what are you doing to yourself? More than likely your health is jeopardized.

Here comes the interesting part. Each of us has a different type and level of fear. Do you know yours? Because it's paramount you know it, deal with it, and release it!

Before we move on to the actual copy creation using fame factors, let's review fear first. It'll be worth it, I promise!

If your business or talent to write sits idle and in fear of succeeding, or failing, or some other reason you've decided is true for you, and you just can't put yourself out there, no amount of expert writing will make you famous!

Fear

Maybe your fear of success was the fame and people's expectations of you...

Well, given this book is about getting famous writing marketing (and other) copy, let's start here first.

What does fear mean exactly? Here are some definitions from the dictionary:

The verb: to fear means...

1) To be afraid of

2) To expect with alarm

3) To be apprehensive

The noun: fear means...

1) An unpleasant, often strong emotion caused by anticipation

or awareness of danger

2) Anxious concern

3) Reason for alarm

4) Painful agitation in the presence or anticipation of danger

5) Loss of courage

Synonyms include: dread, trepidation, fright, alarm and terror. I'm going to break those down... this is important, because if we are going to overcome FEAR, we need to know EXACTLY what it is...

Dread - usually adds the idea of intense reluctance to face or meet a person or situation and suggests aversion as well as anxiety.

Trepidation adds to dread the implications of trembling, and Hesitation.

Fright implies the shock of sudden, startling fear.

Alarm suggests a sudden and intense awareness of immediate Danger.

And Terror implies the most extreme degree of fear.

How to shift from fear-based thoughts to FAITH-based Thoughts

If you have fear-based thoughts, it's because you've been planting fear-based seeds. You need to STOP contaminating your ear gate and eye gate with fear-food and start nourishing your ears and eyes with faith-food.

For example, if you are hearing words through your television, from the internet, in conversations, from the radio, while reading books, or from your own mouth that are drenched in fear, you, your being and your essence, will be drenched in fear.

You are saturating and marinating your mind, body and spirit in fear if you connect yourself with fear-filled words, you'll be filled with fear.

Listen, if you plant rotten seed, fear-based seed – you will get a rotten harvest. Therefore, plant potent, super charged, positive seeds and go turbo–if you really want to make your life amazing, you've got to do things you've never done before!

You've probably heard about those people who were diagnosed with terminal cancer and given five weeks to live. They decided not to do chemotherapy treatment. Instead, they cleaned up their lives from the inside-out.

They followed a turbo regimen eating organic foods, drinking filtered water, exercise, prayer, meditation, fasting, forgiveness, rest, stress elimination, and in weeks the cancer is completely gone and they go on to live a long-healthy life.

Well, some of you have cancerous seeds...causing spiritual cancer and you need a radical, turbo blast regimen of coaching, training, and equipping, combined with support and accountability.

I suggest you hire me as your coach.

Let me plant positive seeds inside your mind and spirit. That's why you bought this book.

You don't have to do it all by yourself.

What I'm teaching you today is not only for you, it's also for someone else—your clients.

My Simple Fear Discovery Process

Now, before we move on, we need to locate and diagnose the fear that you may be possessing. Make a mental commitment right now that you will follow these steps identifying specifically what you fear. Pain is pain, but a headache and a stomach ache are different.

A toothache and a broken arm are different. This exercise will help determine what type of fear you have and to what degree you have it. Then together, we will obliterate it once and for all.

I offer exercises throughout this book. You could call it an interactive book so please participate.

Your Action Plan

Take paper and pen or type on your keyboard the

answers to these questions.

Step #1) If you had a magic wand, what 3-5 breakthroughs would you like to unleash (or begin to unleash) in the next 90 days?

Step #2) How will you feel when you are completely fulfilled in every area of your life (spiritually, physically, socially, financially and

professionally)?

Step #3) What do you believe are the things that have been holding you back from being, doing and having all that you want? In other words, what blocks are draining your energy, causing you stress or preventing you from achieving your goals and living your dream life?

I'll repeat…

What do you believe are the things that have been holding you back from being, doing and having all that you want? In other words, what blocks are draining your energy, causing you stress or preventing you from achieving your goals and living your dream life?

Step #4) What EXACTLY do you fear? Look at your answers from #3 and extract what the fear is. Fear of Success, Fear of Failure, Fear of Rejection, Fear of the Unknown or Fear of Overwhelm? Some or All?

Step #5) What do you NOT LIKE about your situation?

Step #6) What do you LIKE about your situation? If you want to say, "I don't like anything about it…" What's the reward or pay off you get? Please don't skip this step.

It's easy to say, "Oh, I don't like anything about this situation." However, there is something, some type of pay off or some type of reward that is allowing you to keep this situation alive.

Could it be: playing Small to keep you in your "comfort zone" or just barely making ends meet, to keep you in the mentality of '… I know how to manage my life of just barely making-ends-meet type of income – and anything more, will be overwhelming.'

Get the idea?

Remember, you first need to go deep - to rise up, to catapult yourself to the next level – you have to get to the bottom of the fear.

Therefore, don't skip this step!

What's the pay-off of letting fear remain in your life?

Step #7) This is very, very important, so make sure you answer it: How would your life look, if one year from today, you had not made any progress and you were in the exact same place or worse?

Once again, how would your life look, if one year from today, you had not made any progress and you were in the exact same place or worse?

Now, before you answer the question, I want to let you know the reason why I'm asking it in the first place. Ok? It is not to be negative, it's because it is human nature to do more to avoid pain than to gain pleasure. Again, it is human nature to do more to avoid pain than to gain pleasure.

People generally work harder to prevent something bad happening to them, than they do to create something good in their lives. For example, a woman may have built a multi-million-dollar company and if she were about to lose it, she'd work really hard to keep it. Another person is working really hard to create a multi-million-dollar company in the first place. Will she reach it?

Most people will work harder at the former – avoiding the pain as opposed to the latter - gaining the pleasure. Get it?

You may not put as much effort into gaining the pleasure as you would in avoiding the pain.

So…this is a trick question to a degree to get your mind (in a sense), to experience some pain, so that you start to work hard preventing something bad from happening, even though it is for you to gain pleasure. It hasn't happened – we are talking a year from now.

Another reason why I ask this question is because success happens a little bit at a time and so does failure… failure happens a little bit at a time as well.

A lot of people wake up one day and look around, completely dissatisfied with their lives and ask themselves …how did I get here? Well, they got there because they didn't do an exercise like this one, where they looked into the 'crystal ball of their future' so-to-speak…to see where they were headed if they didn't make a change but instead, they continued to do what they were doing on a daily basis. That's how people end up regretting life. I do-not-want-that to happen to you!

What I have found, is that once the pain is identified and then magnified with an accumulated sense of excruciating pain by putting it into the future, (that is why I say one year), clients can see the real impact of their laziness, disorganization, procrastination and fear.

It is important for you to take a hard look at the price your non-action or counterproductive action and fear is costing you.

Answer the question. I know it may not be fun and it may not be comfortable, but please feel the pain as if it really were one year from today and nothing had changed.

And even though you know that you're going to change, do this exercise anyways! OK?

Again, Question #7 (please write this down) is… How would your life look if in one year from today, you had not made any progress and you were in the exact same place or worse?

And please remember, my friend. I have carefully crafted this discovery exercise to cast out fear in your life. So, I urge you to give a hundred percent to this exercise and pretend, just pretend, that your condition did not improve in the next twelve months.

I hope you wrote this down. Because, what you have just described is your future, this is your future…this is your future… unless …you do make some changes and make them fast!

I know it's pretend, but hear me, this scenario is a realistic possibility-for-you if you keep on thinking what you are thinking and doing what you are doing because you are letting fear into your life.

Plain and Simple.

If you keep on thinking what you are thinking and doing what you are doing because you are letting fear into your life, you will be in the exact same place or worse this time next year.

What I'd hate to happen for you is this negative scenario become your reality. Now, here's the good news. This negative scenario that you just imagined is not going to happen because you are reading this book and I'm getting into your head!

I'm helping you take steps to overcome any fear that may prevent you from accepting fame writing copy! Remember-this-negative-scenario, whenever you feel like giving up! Because if you give up, what you just described is what will happen.

Now let's shake off that exercise and get you back into the present moment. Take a moment, stand up and shake your body. Shake off the crud you just thought about. Take a deep breath in, and exhale. Put a big smile on your face and pat yourself on the back. Great job!

Step #8 – the final step of the fear discovery process is to ask yourself, "Why is it a must that I obtain support, accountability and nurturing and make the changes now?"

Now, let's find your fear and get ready to overcome it.

How to Overcome the Fear of Success

To cast out the fear of success, it is imperative that you look as deep as you can into the fear, to completely cast it out.

Like cleaning out a closet, you can't thoroughly clean it out without opening the door and taking a look inside. Fear of success is the same. Open the door, take a look inside, and see what you are dealing with.

Do you have a fear of handling success?

Do you lack the confidence that you'll be able to maintain success once you've achieved it?

Do you fear you'll 'run out of' wisdom or 'run out of' creativity?

Do you fear that once you make it to the top, you'll come crashing down?

Or, do you fear success because you think, "What will I do when

I get 'everything' I want?"

Ask yourself if indeed you have a fear of success. Then dig a little deeper and if yes success is your fear, what exactly do you fear about success?

Pin-point it right now.

How to Prepare for Success

If, for example, you wrote that your fear of success was handling the money. How do you prepare for money now?

Get on top of what you do have. Listen, if you can't keep track of a little bit of money you have now, that little bit of territory you currently have, this could easily be why you are fearing keeping track of having more (because you fear your territory expanding).

Build systems – first externally, such as money tracker systems and second, internally – such as rebuilding your mindset for wealth.

Now, if, for example, you wrote that your fear of success

was bad thinking like, "What will I do when I get "everything I want?"

Make 10-year goals – have lots to look forward to. That way you'll rise up instead of shrinking back.

If you have just a few goals in front of you, you'll have short term vision. If you have years and years' worth of goals, you'll have long-term thinking and won't be worried about "getting everything" once you achieve your next goal.

If, for example, you wrote that our fear of success was because of the demands and responsibilities, change your perspective!

Success is an honor, as well as a duty. You wouldn't be doing this if you didn't believe in your heart that you've been called to succeed. You've been anointed and appointed. You've been raised for such a time as this. Accept it, welcome it and embrace it and also, connect with success through surrendering–pray and meditate—let it go.

This Why I Wrote You This Fame Book

And lastly, if for example, you wrote that your fear of success was the fame and people's expectations of you, you must, I repeat, you must establish boundaries now. Don't wait until you have mobs of people wanting your time and attention. Set up your boundaries and your barriers now!

When you're done here, go back and read what you wrote about why you fear success. Then, using the examples I've given you, take some time to write down how you will prepare for the success you previously feared…

How to Overcome the Fear of Failure

To defeat the fear of failure, you start by digging deep and examining it, then you need to change your perspective and re-define your definition of what it means to fail.

Personally, my definition of failure includes just two items: I don't try, or I quit. That's it. Just two.

If I want to accomplish something and I don't even try, this is failing. And if I want to accomplish something and I quit, when I know that I should stick with it, that's failing!

Anything, again anything, other than not trying or quitting is success to me. Progress is defined as success.

I'll share my definition of success with you – take it: success is progress. As long as I believe this, I am always succeeding! Even if I have a set-back. Make sense? So, take a moment and let's dig deeper. What do you fear about failure? Do any of these statements sound familiar?

I'm not good enough.

I can't do it. It's too difficult.

It will cost too much. I can't afford it. I don't have the money.

It will take too much time, too much effort & too much energy, I will never be able to do it.

I don't have the right credentials, education or experience.

All of the examples I just mentioned are forms of fear, usually called excuses. Sure, they're excuses, however they are rooted in fear.

Now, ask yourself, "Do I have a fear of failure?"

If yes, what exactly do you think failure will look like? Pin-point it right now. Are you ready to move forward in the midst of "failures?"

Get encouragement, go get encouragement because it's not going to come to you. You have to go and get it.

Seek role models, hire coaches, attend seminars, listen to audio

trainings watch video courses, study successful people, read biographies, and most of all, don't wallow in a failure.

My personal secret weapon and the reason why I seldom if ever fear failure is that I focus on helping others succeed. It's the best "fear of failure prevention tactic" I know.

When you are focused on helping others succeed, heal, find peace, even as simple as helping a fellow neighbor rake leaves—doesn't matter, you don't have time to worry about failing! When you focus on the success and healing of others, in addition to your own success and healing, every bit of your being is focused on success and healing. That's the energy you take with you on your next step.

The best way to prevent a "failure" is to combat the paralysis of analysis. Get to work. Go do something.

How to Overcome the Fear of Rejection

To let go of the fear of rejection, it's critical to understand what "rejection" really is. So, to get started, I'd like to go over the definition, so we're all on the same page.

To reject means…

to refuse to accept

to refuse to consider

to refuse to submit to

to refuse to take for some purpose

to refuse to use

to refuse to hear, receive, or admit

to repel

Listen, not everyone on earth will like you or like your ideas. I like to explain this with pies. Some people like to eat apple pie, while others like pumpkin pie. Some like both. And some don't like either.

People have a right to their opinion. But if you make someone else's opinion your business, you then have a recipe for disaster!

If you know in your in your heart of hearts, you make an amazing pumpkin pie, but you're trying to feed it to someone who likes apple pie, you can beat yourself up while begging that person to eat your dessert or you can leave that person alone and go take your pumpkin pie and offer it to someone who actually likes pumpkin pie.

It's all a numbers game. Let's say one in every hundred people do not like you and never will. That would be 1%. Now let's keep the percentage 1%, but let's say you are super successful and more people get to know you. Now you have 100,000 people who are aware of you and your services. 1% of 100,000 is 1,000 people. The percentage is the same, but it's more people.

Who cares? People have a right to their opinion, to dislike something or someone as well as to like something or someone. Personally, I have more people reject me now, then I had ten years ago – because more people know me. This is called math.

On the flip side, more people like me, accept me, respect me and appreciate me now than they did ten years ago. Why? Because more people know me. More people are blessed by me because I'm putting myself out there.

Don't focus on who rejects you, focus on who accepts you. And when someone is mean to you, or says something stupid or lies about you, just remember, that's their problem.

Don't fight fire with fire. If you have haters, let the Universe (God) deal with them. If you need to report them, then do so. If you need to set the record straight, then do so, but don't get down in the gutter with those who come to you covered in filth – false accusations, slander, criticisms, etc. If you start engaging with them, the filth gets on you and in you! The negative energy permeates you too. We want none of that. You have to rise above.

So, take a moment and let's dig deeper. What do you fear about rejection?

Being judged and criticized
Being made fun of and laughed at
Being misunderstood and misinterpreted
Being abandoned, not liked or not accepted
Being hurt

Do you have a fear of Rejection? If yes, what exactly do you fear about rejection?

Pin-point it right now.

How to Prepare for Rejection so you Don't Shrink Back!

Three ways: First of all, understand that God accepts you. (or source, or creator, or whatever you believe spiritually) When you know God loves you, you don't feel hungry nor do you crave for human acceptance. There is nothing more powerful than God's love. But you have to receive it.

Second of all, thank those who accept you. So many times, I see people focus so much of their energy on those who criticize them and then, they pay no attention to those who support them. The more you acknowledge the love and support you have now, the more love and support you'll have.

And thirdly, build your confidence. Personally, when someone rejects me, I feel sorry for them. Because I know that I'm blessed to be a blessing, and if someone doesn't want me to bless them – it's their loss.

Some people could interpret that as arrogant and conceited. Sure, but I interpret it as confident and self-assured.

So, to prepare – understand rejection is all part of the territory. Not everyone will accept you – it's part of life. Also, as you excel and rise up, others will want to pull you down. You can either go down to their level or you can use it as fuel to catapult you to an even higher level.

Use it to fire you up! Use it to strengthen you, to thicken up your skin. Use it for good. You have the power to use rejection to your advantage. Even though I don't enjoy it when people are mean and nasty to me and I prefer supporters and encouragers over haters and critics I've learned to use the hate and criticism to my advantage; it just fuels me.

When someone says I can't do something, I'm like, "Oh yeah? Watch me!"

I admit it used to crush me. On one project, I was called

down and verbally abused because the fellow liked to take pot shots at others. For his personal pleasure. I took almost a year before I stopped having nightmares and crying myself to sleep. I took it personally. So, I finally made a choice to not let it crush me, to let it fire me up instead. I suggest you do the same thing and make that choice right now!

And one more thing – always consider the source. Don't get offended by anyone. But especially, people who are doing worse than you.

When I started my company, I used to allow my feelings to get hurt by people who didn't believe in me, (truth? Even my own husband didn't think I could pull this off. I felt awful) and then I finally realized the hate I was experiencing was from people who didn't believe in themselves.

So, how could they believe in me?

I finally realized, if they have no faith in accomplishing their own dreams, it's no wonder they didn't have faith in me to accomplish my dreams.

So, don't get upset when people hate on you when they are people who aren't who you desire to be like and don't have what you desire to have. Okay?

How to Overcome the Fear of the Unknown

To eliminate the fear of the unknown, it's obvious and easy. Really? Yep. Get to know what you currently define as the unknown. I'll say that again, what exactly do you currently define as unknown?

If the fear is that you don't know something, get to know it. Learn it. Research it. You are the master of your reality. So, get your head out of the sand. And stop letting the unknown rule your life.

My mother worried every day. She worried about the weather and how it would affect our crops. She worried if her children would make it back from school riding a bus for hours each day. All these things were out of her control. Yet, she was strong in so many other ways. She gnashed her teeth; they fell out and she needed dentures. She got sick, a lot!

I grew up with watching her fear the unknown and I vowed not to let it get to me as it did my mother. I knew from an early age that once something is known, it's not unknown anymore. But you don't know if it's going to rain or snow or blow or not tomorrow. You can guess, but for pete's sake, stop worrying about it!

The most common symptoms of the fear of the unknown are: indecision, stagnation, doubt, unbelief and procrastination.

Phew, thank goodness my mother was not a procrastinator. And neither am I. Where there is procrastination, there is always fear. Otherwise it's not procrastination. The definition of procrastination is to put off intentionally the doing of something that should be done.

The reason why you aren't doing something you should be doing, is because you are afraid of something. Don't go day after day, letting fear stop you from going after your goals. Make a decision and go for it. Take action, both mental and physical action. Otherwise you'll feel weak, vulnerable and exposed to more fear.

Every day you let the fear of the unknown fester in your spirit, the weaker you get.

Ask yourself, "Do I have a fear of the unknown"? If yes, what exactly do you fear about the unknown?

Pin-point it right now.

How to Prepare and Look Forward to the Unknown

This is easy - Proverbs 4:7 Wisdom is the principal thing; therefore, get wisdom: and with all thy getting get understanding.

That pretty much wraps it up, I don't need to elaborate. Get proper education.

How to Overcome the Fear of Overwhelm

The fear of overwhelm is also easy to overcome. If, and the key word is if, you get to the root of what you think is overwhelming, it can dissolve almost instantly.

Clarity is key! From my experience, ten out of ten people who tell me, they know that they are called to reach masses through their business and they have a vision, tell me they don't' take enough action because they are tormented with the fear of overwhelm.

If that's you, you lack clarity. You do not have a solid business plan. It's the lack of clarity that is causing the fear.

If you suffer from the fear of overwhelm, I can guarantee, that you have not written your vision and made it as plain and simple step-by-step to follow and check off.

So, take a moment and let's dig deeper. What do you fear about the thought of being in overwhelm?

Growing in your calling, growing your business
Managing and leading people
Dealing with paperwork
Organizing your life
Handling the demands of stepping up
Managing your time effectively

Now ask yourself, "Do I have a fear of overwhelm?" If you answered yes, what exactly do you fear that makes you feel overwhelmed? Pin-point it right now.

How to Prepare for Increase so you Won't Feel Overwhelmed.

Key word is to prepare. If you wrote down that you fear being overwhelmed when you grow your business, grab another piece of paper and write your vision and make it as simple and plain as possible.

If you wrote that you fear managing and leading people, get proper training. Acquire the proper skills so you know what you are doing. Take leadership courses, today.

If you wrote that you fear dealing with paperwork, start streamlining. Implement systems. Hire a professional organizer – get some help.

If you wrote that you fear organizing your life, again, start streamlining now. Listen, it's no wonder when someone fears organizing their life when they think about playing big. But if they can't organize their life while they are playing small, the feat can be overwhelming!

If you wrote that you fear managing your time effectively and handling the demands of stepping up, start cutting off all of the things in your life that you don't need and that are draining your energy. Simply make a list and go down one-by-one, eliminating all of the tasks and responsibilities that you really don't need to be doing.

Decide you will either stop, delegate or do it more efficiently. The main key is to let go of the distractions.

Fear of overwhelm always comes from people who are already overwhelmed and think to themselves, "I can barely get by at the level I'm at now. How am I going to get by-at a higher level with more things to do?"

Apply these steps and get out of the fear of overwhelm. It works.

How to Believe in Yourself, Boost your Confidence and Live a Fearless Life!

If you adopt a fearless attitude, you will, I repeat, you will have victory "as a man thinketh in his heart, so is he". Proverbs 23:7 – it's that simple.

Trust yourself, have faith in your capability regardless of your circumstances– and you'll see your confidence skyrocket and your fear disappear! Stop paying attention to what things looks like or what other people say, and start paying attention to what your inner guidance system says. Go with your gut. Go with what feels good to you. Your feelings are always on point. If you take action feeling fear and uncomfortable, issues will arise. But if you take action feeling good, strong and confident, all manner of greatness occurs.

What YOU Can do to Reduce the Amount of Fear in the World

Walk by faith and not by sight in your own life! Remain calm in difficult situations by keeping your faith strong.

Uplift others. Have faith in others. Hold them able to be do and have what they want. They'll feel your support. Edify, support, encourage and love others. If you have difficulty loving others, at least appreciate some aspect of theirs. Believe in others, lift them up and pray for them.

I know it was content-rich and maybe unexpected in a marketing book. But what so many texts fail to share is, before, during and after the technical training to write good marketing material, comes the inner knowledge you will succeed. And if fears rule, no amount of writing will make your life good. You have to nip fear, increase confidence and now, let's take a short review before we write that fame inducing copy!

Repeat "I Am Famous! I Respect Myself!"

If you think of yourself as worthy, lovable, kind and compassionate, you probably sleep well, eat well, look well, and are generally happy.

You do need to tell yourself the truth about what you really think about yourself.

Ask Yourself, "How Much Do I Believe in Myself?"

Emphasis: If you do not believe you can succeed in your business, you may as well turn around, crawl back under the covers, curl up in a fetal position and stay stuck! You must believe - even for you - the advent of L.A.U.G.H.T.E.R. in your profitable business starts with your attitude.

Now, it's time to get to work. I promise I will not refer to "your attitude" again. I promise:

Your Action Plan

Get quiet and spend a few moments thinking about how you deserve a successful, profitable business. Think about how you would appreciate having customers flocking to your door, or calling you, or emailing you for your service or product. Go back and review your fear that's ready to be let go.

Think about how you will feel when you achieve the level you desire you wish to reach. Imagine the big picture result of your success and actually set a date to achieve it. (three months, three years…)

If you're hesitating a fraction, know that this exercise is no different than creating a business or financial plan. Your banker needs both – so do you.

If for any reason, you start to think about how it won't work, say this next phrase out loud.

"Up till now I thought (insert any fear or doubt, or negative ideas about your business, service, product or you).

Now I know (insert your positive statement about the success of your venture).

Thank you and please make this or something better happen in ways that are for the highest good of me and of everyone else involved."

Repeat the phrase each time any negative thoughts creep in. Honor those negative thoughts because they once served you. Now, you can release the amount of power they hold on you. Deflate the fear as you would a rubber raft!

How to Get into A Right Write Mindset

Now that we've ruled out fear, let's begin. What we are doing up to now is establishing an energy or sense of confidence before the actual writing. Why?

Long sales copy still works, even in this age of five-second attention spans and mile-a-minute marketing messages. But to hold your reader's attention, every sentence must have something important to say. To guarantee you hold your reader's attention, you must muster the confidence about your product, service, business, or about you, to a level that is felt from here to well... you decide.

Keep the "information and energy density" high by considering this simple 4 P formula:

Promise: Tell the reader how he will come out ahead by becoming your customer.

Picture: Help the reader visualize the benefits.

Proof: Prove that you can deliver the benefits.

Push: Ask for the order.

(Source: The Complete Idiot's Guide to Direct Marketing, Bob Bly)

Your Action Plan

Take a pen and piece of paper out. Jot down your ideas to these three important strategies:

Customer Service -- How can you satisfy your customer, so they want to continue business with you?

Education/motivation/training -- **Sales begin with you.** If you are not personally sold on your company and its products then your customers (and your staff, by the way) are not convinced to buy! Put another way: **If you are not at ease with your sales abilities -- neither will your customers be at ease buying from you!**

Effective Customer Support -- How long do you want to be in business? Answer this truthfully, and then ask yourself, can you change and go with the flow if necessary?

You must write such good sales information as to have your customers follow your "way of thinking". It must answer those five major questions that your customer has in her head. It must satisfy her needs. It must influence your customer so much that her "most natural response" will be to purchase your product or service.

Have I scared you? Successful businesses do this. It has been done. And now it's your turn.

It's up to you to shed light on the problem.

Your Action Plan

Repeat the above exercise about ... **Up till now**.... if you need to.

Bonus 1: Self-esteem Builder: The next time you hear yourself saying, "I can't..." substitute it with "I'm unwilling to because..."

Bonus 2: Self-esteem Builder: Whenever you hear yourself exclaiming, "I have to..." substitute with "I get to..."

I guarantee you will notice a change in your demeanor.

Now let's go to the next module. Identify and apply a process you can clearly define, support and preserve, reestablish, upgrade and repeat every possible way, all the time, at every place, with anyone!

Anyone?

OK, maybe not anyone, however definitely...

Your customer!

5. A—ADDRESS YOUR AUDIENCE

I've seen plenty of data to support the idea that you can make $100 an hour or more simply by specializing in an area you already know. If you are a doctor, you can develop a specific area of expertise and teach it to others in your field. If you are a plumber or an architect or an accountant, you can do the same.

You can work for a salary for the rest of your life and grow wealthy slowly ... or you can become an expert in your field, make at least as much money as you do now, and work a lot less.

You can target the customer who needs your specialization or product.

You can do this if you know how. **You can do this** when you narrow down to your specific audience, your specific niche, and your specific specialization.

Yes, you must be willing to specialize and offer your unique product, service to also a specialized audience and **capture their attention**.

You can develop top-notch expertise in some special area of your industry. You can do that, and what's more... you can learn how to sell yourself. But all that will take a little time. And that's why you need to start now -- so that you can make the transition when you're ready.

How Do You Target Your Niche Market?

Think about the industry you're in now. Who gets paid the most? What kinds of problems cause the most trouble? What types of opportunities produce the greatest profits? Narrow it down and get your target.

However, there's a catch.

If you spend countless hours and hundreds of pages planning your new business venture, you are wasting a lot of time. That's mostly because you don't know the most important secrets about your target market.

What's Most Critical About Any Customer Need Is Usually Invisible at First

No amount of planning or preparation is going to change this. The key to being successful is having a good general idea of what you want to do. However, **be flexible enough to change plans quickly** as you discover the invisible secrets of the market you've jumped into.

Discover the Invisible Target Market Secrets

I mentioned business and financial plans. It's time to go into more detail.

Experts have recommended that business plans be limited to four pages. An article in the Harvard Business Review on entrepreneurship provides a structure that works well for such a pared-down proposal.

The structure, suggested by Harvard Professor William A. Sahlman, is based on the idea that there are four factors critical to the success of every new venture.

- The people
- The opportunity

- The context
- The risk/reward ratio

Asking and answering specific questions can approach each of these factors.

The People

- Who will you use?
- What do they know?
- Who do they know?
- How well are they known?

A huge mistake writers of marketing copy make is to assume that your prospective customer knows what you're talking about. This is especially true in social media where you only have a few words or phrases to make your point.

That means you use big words, you use industry jargon and assume a level of education or understanding that just isn't there.

An example is using online acronyms like SEO, which by the way, means search engine optimization. Yet you see a lot of people chatting up about it! To most of your customers, that sounds like Charlie Brown's teacher "Wha wha wha."

And because more than 50% of people are now viewing you online through smart phones, you really have to get to speed what they know and understand! Too easy to click you out!

What you have to do is write for the lowest common denominator in your audience because then you can't go wrong and you won't offend people. I like to advice people to write at least a grade 7 average. This meets the needs of educated and non-educated customer types.

The Opportunity

Your plan should profile your business itself (what it will

sell and to whom) and answer the following questions:
- Is the market sufficiently large and growing at an acceptable rate?
- Is the industry/sector structurally attractive?

The Context

Sahlman suggests you look at the big picture – the regulatory environment, the demographic and market trends, economic factors, etc. These are usually factors that are beyond the control of the people engaged to run the business. Questions of context should include:
- What can happen that could sink the business?
- Are there any contextual problems you haven't thought?

The Risk/Reward

The "risk/reward" questions must take into account everything that can go wrong, assess the damage that might be caused, and discuss how the team could respond. On the positive side, ask
- How big can this get?

Here are additional considerations for each:
- The opportunity: What market niche does this fill? How will it help your customers? How much money can you make?
- The people: Who can run this? Who can provide advice? Who are the leading experts in this area? How can you create a network that will ensure success?
- The risks and costs: How much will it cost you? How much if everything doesn't work out? What are the legal and regulatory risks? What are the opportunity and distraction costs?
- Plan B Scenario: What do you do if it doesn't work out? How can you limit losses and recoup a reasonable portion of the resources invested?

You've probably thought this entire process through already so forgive me for rambling on. However, it is so important to be absolutely clear about your business intentions. This makes all the difference in how you write your marketing information materials. Your clarity (or lack of) actually reflects in your written copy as attitude -- oops. Sorry I promised I wouldn't mention attitude!

Let's focus on the customer now -- your buyers.

Your Action Plan
Stage One: Determining the Qualities of Your Customer
Step #1

At the top of a sheet of paper, please write the title: 'The Qualities of My Customer Are ...'

Step #2

Think of someone you know who fits your customer profile. Who is it that would benefit and surely buy from you?

Under this title, list all of the positive qualities, characteristics, attributes, and talents that you would want your perfect customer to possess. Give yourself at least five minutes to make a complete list.

Step #3

Review what you have written. Did you forget any positive qualities? Be sure not to let anything go without saying. Add them all to the list.

Step #4

Put down your pencil.

Step #5

Now ask yourself...Is there anything more that I would want my customer to be that would make him or her even better? Perhaps you would like them to visit your web site more often, or you would like them to spend a larger amount of money on your products or services, or you would like them to refer their friends to you.

Go ahead. Ask for the impossible! What could it hurt?

Step #6

Pick up your pencil and add any of the following positive qualities to your list.

Feel free to use the following list of qualities as inspiration for your list of qualities:

They keep their appointments with me.

They trust that I have their best interests at heart.

They already have a growing business.

They are intelligent and practice good common sense.

They have a strong network of friends and associates they refer.

They have a financial cushion to pay me.

They pay on time and up front.

They make me feel like a guru.

They support me in attracting ___ contracted clients each month.

They understand and demonstrate they deserve to be successful.

They want to work with a coach and me.

They make a request to become my client.

They value their and my time.

They have a sense of humor.

They love to pay me.

They provide me with repeat business.

They are peaceful, calm, and kind.

They want me to be successful and make a profit.

They have offices in great locations around the country.

They have a high-margin, high-volume business.

They always say thank you.

They have and demonstrate integrity, loyalty and consistently.

They have realistic expectations of what can be achieved by when.

They want me to work only from _a.m. -_p.m. Tuesday through Thursday.

They personally guarantee the contracted agreement with me.

They provide me with 5 referrals each in a 6-month period.
They have clarity.
They are collaborative.
They treat everyone like they are special.
They are sincere.
They have the same value system and work ethic as I do.
They are open-minded.
They are reliable.
They praise me to anyone and everyone.

Stage Two: 'What's Your Customer's Core Emotional Desire?'

When we have knowledge of our customers' and clients' missions and motivations, we are able to relate to our customers as vibrant people who have as much at stake in the success of our business as we do.

This is where synchronicities start. In order to know what makes your customer tick, you must first know what makes you tick.

The Law of Attraction, from which the scientific law such as cause and effect draws its power, ensures that 'like attracts like.' If you need to, go back to Chapter 3 and Science 101 to refresh your mind about the Law of Attraction.

Interestingly, what makes us tick is also what makes our customer tick.

Please return to the sheet of paper on which you just wrote the list of the qualities of your perfect customer. After this list (or on another sheet of paper) write the title 'What's My Customers Core Emotional Desire?'

Then, put your pencil down.

Now, please allow yourself as much time as you need (all day if necessary) to consider and focus on how you would answer the following questions:

Why do you get out of bed in the morning?

What is most important to you in the world?
What do you want to achieve before you leave this world?
What do you really love about your life?

At the end of this day, arrive at *one* sentence in answer to the question:

"What is the most important thing in the world to me?'

Write this *one* sentence under the title "What's My Customer's Core Emotional Desire?"

(Source: Adapted from *Attracting Perfect Customers,* Hall & Brogniez)

Congratulations! You've now set the Right Energy in motion to write your sales material. You now have someone very specific to write your promotion to.

In event you think this is a ridiculous exercise, I want to share what Vince Lombardi once said, and "Confidence is contagious. So is lack of confidence." I think you get the big picture.

6. U—UNIQUE ABOUT YOU?

"I approached this letter as I would any direct-mail sales letter. It was hard initially 'writing about my stuff' I think most people are like that, but especially non-writers. I got over that block simply by focusing that my business was the only way to success." – Author Unknown

Knowing your customer is key. However, knowing what your customer will gain from having your unique product is equally important.

What does your customer need? What makes your customer tick? What emotions could you touch with your promise? How could you make your customer's life easier, better, less stressful?

Your letter has to say 'buy me' better than any of your competitor's promotions. You want your customer to feel you could be the best thing for her or him. You want her to feel she had nothing to risk in trying you.

Here's a quick summary to consider while writing the bulk of your sales letter:

Don't be apprehensive about writing good things about yourself. Keep it at a minimum. You have to believe in your product. Sell your best features through benefits.

Approach the letter as you would any sales letter. Know your customer. How can you benefit her? What emotions can you hit? What can you promise? In other words, understand your core intention.

Start. Ask for the opportunity to solve a problem she has, but stay away from the stuff the competition is already doing.

Make an offer the client cannot refuse . . . because she has nothing to lose. This probably means giving some sort of guarantee initially - what works for you?

Clearly delineate the benefits and your USP. If you haven't figured out your USP, let's do it now.

Take your time . . . and do it right. You will not get a second chance once your customer reads your promotion.
Unique Selling Proposition (USP) – What's unique about you?

A colleague shared this story. I like to use it as an example, however extreme it may seem. It illustrates the concept of USP.

This Successful Butcher Sells Hugs!

Think about the meat cutting business for a moment – price is typically how they advertise and compete. Yet, most people will pay a little more if given a good reason to. If you are hosting a special dinner party – the price of the meat is not your main concern – it is what the end result of the meal is. If your guests rave about it being the best they have ever had – then you are happy. And you are willing to pay a premium to guarantee the meal is the best they ever had.

A Success Story

Ten years ago, Lori scraped together her savings to attend a seminar being put on by Ted Nicholas (a direct marketing master and copywriting genius). She got his attention during the break and told him this story.

She and her husband had been struggling with maintaining their butcher shop (almost to the point of closing the doors), because the entire parking lot was ripped up and unusable for 6 months – totally destroying their customer flow.

So how could she get more customers in?

Ted started asking some questions and found out that her husband was quite a tall man, and he loved to hug people.

How One Single Piece Of Advice Turned Their Lives Around

He said "when you get back home – first thing I want you to do is call your butcher shop "The Hugging Butcher" – advertise it everywhere, new signs and all over your marketing. Use direct response style marketing and make that husband of yours the hugging butcher. Have him stand at the front door and hug everyone that walks through – men, women and children."

She followed Ted's advice precisely. Quicker than she ever could have dreamed – business was booming! People couldn't wait to visit the hugging butcher – business went through the roof (despite the unfinished parking lot).

Soon, they were able to raise the price and commanded the highest price in the market they served – and clients lined up at the door. After a few years they sold that business for a very large sum of money – amazing what a simple differentiation can do for a business!

Having just said that – a mistake you don't want to make is to write garbage! If it's boring, all about you, egocentric, featureless and no benefits, you'll lose them!

Make sure your copy is all about your customer's needs and solves their problems. You know the difference between good copy and garbage. Don't put it out over on your own website, social media or advertising brochures!

Your Action Plan

Take a piece of paper and first, just sit quietly for a moment. Answer these questions.

Why is my product better than others like it?

What can it give to my customers that no other product can?

Is this product what my customer really needs?

Go ahead and make your answers lengthy. By that I mean, list at least 10 items per question. Take your time.

Now, pull out the most significant item from question 1, 2 and 3. Put them together in a phrase or statement. This is your USP.

The value for the customer, the difference from the competitor and the belief you have exactly what the customer needs.

Rational Deliverance Isn't Enough

Actually, this is a review about energy.

Your marketing material probably has all the markings of a rational deliverance – all kinds of profound and provocative principles and techniques as well as dimensions, weights and measures.

However, we've already agreed that the energy in the promotions is the key to sales.

Here's something interesting. People don't like to be sold (they like to buy things, but they don't like to be sold). Second, *people buy for emotional, not rational reasons* – so you have to appeal to your prospects' feelings and desires.

(Source: AWAI Six Figure Copywriting Program)

Not surprisingly, once they are sold, then people need to justify the irrational decisions with rational reasons. So at what point do they respond and become your loyal customer?

Are you running in circles here?

Well let's clarify a few things.

If you're thinking to yourself right now, "Hmmff. Well,

I certainly can't understand how somebody can't see the "logic" of just how valuable this product (or service) is to them..." you're missing the boat and not approaching this from the emotional context.

In fact, reread the above statement Hmmff. Notice the attitude? If yours is similar guess what you are infesting into your marketing material! Attitude. And your customer senses it. They stay away!

All right... I'm done about attitude!

7. G—GET PROOF AND GIVE PROOF

Are you satisfying your customers?

How would you know if your customer was happy with your product, service and general business conduct? How would you know if she's satisfied?

Do you care?

Of course, you do, otherwise you wouldn't be in business to serve your customer, nor would you be reading this book.

When a potential customer first visits you, or buys from you, are you getting her name, email and postal addresses? Very few companies do – yet they complain about lackluster sales. This represents an effective form of networking – a valuable process to get to know your customer.

Your best source of new profits will be your client and prospect list.

Get those names! No matter what business you are in – offer them an incentive to give you their names.

For example, one wine supply store never collected the names of its customers. They had almost 400 people come in each month. When they collected those names and sent out promotions for special events, sent emails, letters and miraculously, those same customers returned twice and three times in the same month! That's 300% increase in sales volume!

Then people started coming from across the province not just within the city. Word got around this was a "sensitive to their needs" kind of kit and supply store. Home Wine Makers wouldn't go anywhere else.

Do you send mailers with free samples or special coupons?

The other thing they did was follow up with their best customers.

A phone call always works well however it may not work for you. Remember, if you're uncomfortable, that energy transfers – so you might hire an outside firm to phone. Here are some other suggestions you could offer:

Special offers

First chance of purchase for preferred customers

Limited viewing times for new products

Free bonuses

Surveys

Tips and techniques to use your products more efficiently

Asking them to come in, as it has been some time since they visited

This is one area you cannot go wrong with. As long as you have something worthwhile to share with them – they will appreciate it. And they will show you their appreciation in the form of sales and profits.

Where to Get Leads For Your Business

Fewer than 5% of the businesses in existence today do this – any wonder why fewer than 5% last more than ten years? What is it?

Get leads! Get Email addresses!

First and foremost, the best place to find your leads is to find them where your ideal customers are.

Many business owners stumble around blindly trying to

place ads wherever they can – without two minute's worth of thought or research into the feasibility of that magazine or newspaper.

First you must really understand your ideal client base, but how?

Ask them! Survey them – and make sure you make it worth their time out of their day to answer your survey. Structure the survey so you find out where they shop, what they read (magazines, newspapers, niche magazines, and trades magazines – anything you can find out), where they spend their weekends, if they volunteer anywhere, do they have kids? What ages? Find out everything you possibly can about them.

Find commonalties in places they frequent, what they read, shows they watch, ages of their kids – anything that appears more frequently than others – note it as it will pay for itself on thousand times over.

And yes, this does take time to do.

Only 5% Ask!

You do not know what your customer wants! Yet 95% of business owners THINK they know but have never asked. And you are almost always wrong if you are not asking.

Ok, now you know of some common interests. Start phoning around to the newspapers, magazines, trade magazines, newsletters, etc. – ask to get their media kits.

Media kits show the demographics of their readers, circulation numbers, average incomes, male/female, and a lot of other assorted information that will also be helpful. The media kit shows how much various style ads cost. Excellent information for you.

What you are looking for is high circulation numbers, targeted to your perfect clients – and low advertising pricing.

Here's the real reason only 5% collect leads!

You need to have a reason for people to give you their contact information, so you can then follow up.

It can be a free report, a free white paper, or a video series or audio or combination free webinar. It needs to be something cool and they'll want enough to give up their name and email, otherwise you're not building a business; you're just running a promotion.

You could also get them to go to your Facebook Fan page, join a Facebook group, like you LinkedIn, or follow you on Twitter.

These things can happen after you collect names!

There are other ways to entice your visitors to subscribe to your newsletter or free offer.

The number 1 decider between success and failure is a very good title. So remember, whatever you are offering, it has to sound simple yet exciting.

Your Action Plan
Determining The Type Of Copy To Write

You could develop a print media strategy, complete with magazines, newspapers and trade magazines that you can advertise in continually. You could also have a variety of ads you can run, and rotate amongst them (with tracking numbers on each on to measure the effectiveness of each ad in each advertising medium).

Your Website Pages Are Ads!

Test lots of different media, letters, brochures, lots of different ads, and ad sizes. Find the winner ads, the winner publications etc. Then test those winner ads in unusual places or untested publications.

This may surprise you! You may find the hidden gold nuggets in some unusual places when you start looking and testing.

I want to repeat here, your website pages – plural – are

ads. Even your About Us Page, and Your Testimonials are opportunities to apply direct response and ask for what you want!

The best use of copy is on every single blog post you write! That's right – blog!

Every site needs updated content. It's now enough to have a page that sells your products or services. You don't get ranking or get your website up to the first page in searches if you don't create content on a regular basis.

Even if you change up a header, a paragraph or create a blog post as rarely as monthly, you need updated content to be considered a legitimate site. And a blog makes it the easiest and covers your bases for SEO (search engine optimization)

Direct Mail is still the best lead generation media of all.

Write 50! Write 100 ads!

Once you find which examples of winning ads that pull in the most leads at the cheapest price – your direct mail system can continue chugging along, generating cash on a regular basis, every single time you are running ads.

Here are some tools you can use in your direct mail campaign: postcards, 4 page letters, booklets, one page ads, oversized (sumo) postcards, tear sheet mailers (you can hire companies that will rip the edges of your mailers to look like it came out of a magazine – ask your printer about this). There are many forms of direct mail.

Bonus 1: Test out alternative media as well – credit card stuffers, package inserts, card decks, coupon booklets like Val-Pak. All of these are very worthy of tests to see what response you can get. All it takes is one that hits the target market and you will have a miniature gold mine at your disposal.

And don't forget social media! Facebook has close to 4.5 Billion people liking and connecting every single day!

Advertise for as little as $10 a day and increase your presence online!

Whew! That's a lot of networking and question asking and writing! Welcome aboard!

Give Proof: Credibility, Statistics and Testimonials

This is as important as any benefit. Find someone who uses your company and ask them to give you a testimonial.

Three to five relating specifically to the area you are selling have proved to work well relieving hesitation, customer remorse and healthily confirm validity.

The fact is your customer does not want to be the first to try your product or service. So you must give her proof that other extremely satisfied customers have used your products and services first.

Offer testimonials, statistics, credentials and expert testaments. Show graphs, pictures, diagrams and evidence to support your claims.

8. H—HEADLINE: YOUR BEST FRIEND

Headlines! Here's how they target your customer.

"The odds of hitting your target go up dramatically when you aim at it."-- Mel Pancoast

Sounds simple. However, how accurate are you focused on targeting your ideal customer? Are you sending the appropriate "first impression"?

Let's say for example, at any given point in time, there are a number of potential customers viewing your web site, reading your advertisement, or hearing about you from someone who was pleased with your service or product.

It won't be easy to convince them to take you seriously -- unless you can find a way to **aim directly** at the ones who will buy what you sell.

How can you do this? By way of your opening, or **Headline**, that gets them hooked.

Have you ever visited a web site & found yourself wondering what to click on?

Telegraph Your Messages

Every page should have a headline shouldn't it? What's

more, it should have a photo as well displaying what that page content is all about!

A headline and subheads telegraph the benefits that your customer can expect.

Studies prove that if a web site visitor doesn't find something that engages her interest in 6 seconds or less, she's out of there. Never make the all too common assumption that your prospects are going to carefully examine, consider, or navigate the content on your web site just because it's there.

This is true for all other promotion styles. You letter needs a headline to grab attention as well.

Remember this; your customers will consider you only when you target their **very deep desires**. You have to gratify their most important needs. Instantly! Up front.

The truth is, they will not wait around to learn how you can help them solve their problems, make them richer, or offer them your expertise in exactly the area they need most. They need to know right up front.

The Most Important Feature On Your Promotion

So give them a powerful benefit laden headline. Your headline is *the* most important thing about any web page, or for that matter any form of media, including all forms of advertising, editorial, press release, signage, letters, a restaurant menu, you name it.

It doesn't matter how good the main body of the message is, if nobody reads it.

What Makes A Great Headline?

Let me give you a couple of hints.

A good headline is about your customer's needs being met.

A great headline feels like it's exactly what the customer needs to hear right now.

A great headline enters the heart of the 'emotional target'

A powerful headline makes the customer nod her head and want to read more – intrigued to go further.

A powerful headline fulfills and leaves no doubt about how she can benefit from reading the main body of the text.

Then there are a few more points to consider:

Size does matter. Larger and bolder headlines grab attention better than smaller ones.

The least expensive print costs are black and white. However, if your letter takes on the form of a brochure or web page, use color. Color adds impact. Blues and pastels are relaxing while orange and reds are bolder.

Include a photo. This way the headline 'sounds' like it comes from that expert.

Stay away from too much graphics; make it plain and simple – a strong emotion-filled statement.

I've studied, read about and used over a dozen different styles. To be honest, most of my headlines were similar – I realized I used these 3 basic, yet powerful headline techniques. I'm sure you'll agree:

Benefit style headlines offer one main practical benefit of the product.

"Burn Disease Out of Your Body
-Lying flat on your back, using nothing more
than the palm of your hand."

It's important however not to be a copycat. Make sure the benefit you're offering is truly unique - or presented in a very unique and intriguing way. Get creative.

A wonderful example is this John Carlton's powerful headline:

"Amazing Secret Discovered by
One-Legged Golfer
Adds 50 Yards to Your Drives, Eliminates Hooks and Slices
... and Can Slash Up to 10 Strokes From Your Game Almost Overnight"

Emotions packed headlines directly address the emotional need, frustration, or fear that the product's primary benefit addresses. This is one Clayton Makepeace wrote and won awards for:

7 HORSEMEN OF THE COMING
STOCK MARKET APOCALYPSE:
These 7 emerging crises have now GUARANTEED that the most painful stock crash of your lifetime is STILL AHEAD!

Then answer in point form, why. Give a list of proof, a list of benefits to qualify your claim.

"Let me give you the secrets of FEARLESS CONVERSATION!"
"I promise you the ability to walk into a room full of strangers-and talk to anyone with total confidence, authority and flair."

Suppose you were selling a headache remedy. "How Do Doctor's Cure Their Own Headaches?" Doesn't this appeal to one of your greatest human needs? Curiosity.

Do you think you'd invest a few more minutes to find out by reading the rest of the copy?

A great headline takes advantage of human emotion.

Suppose you were selling maternity clothing. "How To Present Yourself Fashionably, One Belly At A Time". You'd be thinking, Hmm, I wonder what kind of maternity fashion would look good?

A good headline is NOT about you! It's NOT "We Have the Highest Quality Merchandise, with Great Service Selection, & Everyday Low Prices"! As consumers, aren't we bombarded by this kind of relentless platitude all day long, day in and day out? Enough!

Appeal to their human instincts in your headlines and copy, and watch your business grow! But don't try to reinvent the wheel.

Your Action Plan
The Most Effective Selling Words

Here are 39 most effective words in the English language

for writing powerful headlines. It is recommended that you use them in your web, letter and e-mail newsletter headlines:

Special Note: Due to a high volume of SPAM, especially generated through e-mail campaigns, specific words (*) automatically cause the entire information to be filtered out - choose your words wisely if you want your customer to receive your copy. This particularly applies to e-mails.)

Fr*e*e, Guaranteed, New, Your, You, Introducing, Easy, Mon*e*y, Discover, Results, Proven, Love, Benefits, Save, Alternative, Now, Sa*le, W*in, Gain, Trustworthy, Good Looking, Comfortable, Proud, Healthy, Safe, Val*ue, Right, Way, Win*nin*gs, Fun, Advice, Wanted, Announcing, People, Most, Effective, Strategy, Happy.

9. T—TIGHTEN THE CONTENT

It's time to put words to paper.

Write. Yes, write. Take as long as you wish. First you may want to list out all ideas you have based on the information you collected so far.

The key here is to write like you speak -- conversationally. Pretend you are explaining what you have for sale to someone who is interested in buying. How would your conversation go? How would you "persuade" them this is the best solution to their perceived problem? How will they benefit by using you?

Not "To Be!"

Remember the first rule of good conversation -- and the most important one -- eliminate all forms of the verb "to be."

Verbs are "action words" and the common forms of the "to be" verb include is, are, was, were, and am.

You want your copy to be lively, exciting, and visual. You want your prospect to imagine a vivid, compelling picture. The way to do this is to use strong, active verbs. And "to be" verbs are not active. They are weak and passive.

Try this mental test: Visualize the word "jump." That's not too difficult. Maybe you thought of a basketball player making a jump shot or your child jumping off the diving board.

Now, visualize the verb "is" . . . or "am" . . . or "was." That's not so easy, is it?

Let's take this one step further. You can develop an even stronger image by using verbs that are more descriptive. Imagine Michael Jordon "soaring" toward the basket. Or a child "leaping" off the high dive. The point is, when you get away from using forms of the verb "to be," you open up a whole, rich world of verbs that convey a huge range of actions and imagery.

Your Action Plan

I'm going to give you five sentences using forms of "to be." Change these verbs to lively, more powerful, active verbs. (Hint: when you change the verb, you'll probably want -- or need -- to change other words in the sentence too.)

I've listed a suggestion for each sentence at the end of this section article -- but keep in mind that there are no correct answers. Your changes might be much better than mine.

OK, here are the five sentences:

Lister Hall is on top of the hill.

Steve Small is a successful banker.

SymcoTechno stock was down 312 points.

Polycosanol is a good LDL cholesterol-lowering natural substance.

The fall colors are brilliant.

Of course, you cannot eliminate "to be" verbs completely. Some are indispensable. (Like the one I just used.) But if you want to strengthen your copy significantly, go on a "search and destroy mission" to weed out as many of the "to be" offenders as you can.

Word Hunt at The End

One more very important suggestion: Don't go on this word hunt when you're writing the first draft of your copy. When you're creating your first draft, let the ideas rip. Don't slow your creative juices by trying to edit at the same time. The best time to do it is in your second draft.

How well did you do with rewriting the above sentences?

Here are some suggestions on ways to eliminate "to be" verbs:

Lister Hall stands guard over the Saskatchewan River

When it comes to picking successful stocks, Steve Small kicks butt! (OK, maybe you wouldn't say this in a promo -- then again, maybe you would).

SymcoTechno stock plummeted 312 points.

Polycosanol lowers LDL cholesterol significantly -- and naturally.

In the fall, nature paints the mountains using a palette of yellows, gold, and brilliant crimsons.

Your Action Plan
Documentation Clean-Up: Editing & Polishing

Let's say for a moment, your manuscript, letter, report or your simple e-mail is almost done.

There are the housekeeping details to take care of. Why?

Clean Documentation Accomplishes Three Important Goals

It makes your readers happy. Happy readers are less likely to nit-pick their way through your information. That means fewer rewrites and revision for you -- particularly if the information you send is for review and you get it back. However, if the information is final, you've lost your chance of making an impression if you have errors in your draft. When was the last time you read a piece of literature that had spelling errors? How did it make you feel? Critical? Judgmental? Just imagine how your reader might think of you and your work if it's sloppy.

It helps solidify your reputation as a true professional. That, along with meeting deadlines and keeping appointments, submitting error-free information will pretty much give you license to get what you ask for.

It ensures that your work is virtually error-free. You'll be much less likely to have "embarrassing errors" slip through the cracks -- and show up in your final submission.

Tricks to Polished Documents

The first thing you should do is absolutely nothing.
That's right -- *nothing!*
You've just finished writing your important documentation. Now you need to put it away for a while. Two days should do it for the big, important pieces. And even if it's a reply to an e-mail, a minute away can save you embarrassment.

Why? Because it's almost impossible to look objectively at your work you've just written. Your eye is more likely to see what you *meant* to say instead of what's actually on the paper.

So take a break. You deserve it!

Once you've taken a step back from your work, you'll be amazed at how many little errors you'll find. You'll see where you wrote "you" when you meant "your"..."your" when you meant, "you're"..."there" that should be "their" ... "it's" that should be "its" ... and so on.

You'll also find that sentences you thought flowed beautifully are really stiff and awkward. Don't worry. It happens to all of us. And you'll be amazed at how a few hours of editing will make your report sing.

To ensure that your written work is squeaky clean, I recommend this foolproof system I learned as a professional copywriter...

Copy Cleaning System

Read your documentation out loud. Start at the top. Read every word. (Tape record yourself doing it if you like, particularly if your career is on the line and it's longer than five pages!)

Sounds crazy but, reading aloud does two very important things. First, it forces you to read every word slower than if you were reading it to yourself.

Second, it helps you catch awkward and "twisted" phrasing. Sentences that don't naturally roll off your tongue. Words that are difficult to pronounce. Phrases too long to say in one breath. Remember that good writing is 99% conversational writing. You're communicating your ideas with someone.

Note: If your writing doesn't sound like you're talking to your best friend, it's not good copy. (Some variations to this rule, notwithstanding, of course).

If you need an example of the way your work should read, take a look at the way I've written this information for you. Sentences flow. The tone is conversational. Paragraphs are nice and short.

After you've read your work out loud and have corrected the entire clumsy wording, it's time for Copy Cleaning Step #2.

Proofread every sentence of document -- from the bottom on up.

This one is a piece of cake. Proofread your document, beginning with the very last sentence and working backwards.

With this method, you're much more likely to catch errors. That's because when you're reading backwards, it's much more difficult for your eye to jump ahead. Therefore, your concentration is on spelling, punctuation, grammar, and so forth.

That's it! **Oh, one more thing**. Depending on the importance of the information, you may want to do this step, just in case...

Let Others Read It.

Use your discretion here of course. However, having another set of eyes, 2 sets are even better, you're sure to get the feedback your report deserves.

Hire me as your proofreader! Not only do I write copy, I am a trained and certified proofreader. You're looking for overall "broad-stroke" comments. So you give your report or important documentation to at least two people and ask them to review it. Me included!

You can ask anyone you want. It can be your colleague, spouse, a friend, your mother, your father, brother or sister. Just ask them to read the document as you've written it.

Ask them about structure, spelling, but more importantly, appeal. Will it persuade, instruct, advice, or do what your original intention is? Ask them where within the structure its weakest and where they see a need to rewrite.

Again, this is a valuable step if what you are sending is extremely important to receive positive response. Don't be afraid to check it out first.

There you have it -- basic foolproof and effective proof reading. And never forget to send your computer-generated information through the Spell Checker!

We're bridging the gap between you and your customer.

Engage Your Imagination... then take it where you will. Where the mind has repeatedly journeyed, the body will surely follow. People go only to places they have already been in their minds. And now...

10. E—ENGAGE THEIR EMOTIONS

What area gave you the most grief?
I'll bet it was the benefits! Benefits are what engage emotions.

Well let's go over this again, which is the one concept the hardest to grasp.

Your Action Plan

You already know the features and description of your product. You already know what it can do for your customer.

But answer this: "What's in it for her?" (Your customer) Then ask, "So What?" Confusing? Let's try a few examples.

Let's say you wrote in your copy that your Carrot Top Peeler is 3 times sharper than a standard carrot peeler on the market.

Your customer asks herself, "So What?"

You think this through and add; well... she will spend less time peeling carrots because she wouldn't have to go over previously peeled areas.

"So What?"

She'll have more time to spare.

"So What"?

Well, she'll have 2 more hours each week to spend with her family.

"So What?"

"Her husband will feel closer to her and remember that she is available for him.

"So Wh… great! That's more like it.

When you can't ask "So What?" that's a benefit. Write it into your copy beside the relevant feature it belongs to and in a bullet benefit list in the copy. **Capture her attention and she is "moved" to buy.**

This is the power of benefit persuasion.

Do this with all the features you know about your product, service, any business idea you want to promote. This works like a charm!

The Most Common Reason Customers Don't Buy!

Before I share the reason, I want to tell you a story.

It was a windy, overcast, blustery Saturday morning when a group of us met for our annual golf tournament. Not everyone played well. In fact, not everyone played before.

But it's not about the golf that I want to share. It's about my looking foolish. I'm sure each of you has your own golf story. In fact, golf is probably the most obvious example of how people just don't like looking foolish – and when they do – they get very, very – well, you've probably seen it! What I want to share is what happened after the game.

We finally ended the fiasco tournament, cold, grumpy, noses running, and hands purple and numb. We got to go home! I was tired and still miserable when I decided I just had to stop into the grocery store first. What a dumb idea. Did I mention I was tired?

After purchasing 2 items, I was ready to head home. As I was turning right to exit the parking lot, I heard a foreboding scraping sound. I stopped, got out my vehicle and to my horror; I realized I cut too close to the cement pillar marking the corner of the lot. My running board was scraped, but not so bad.

I got back into my vehicle and looked up into the rearview mirror. Standing there with grins on their faces were two total strangers watching me make a fool of myself. Yes, that's what I thought. They think I'm a fool!

What I did next, I regret with all my heart.

I felt the blood rush up my neck and into my brain. Something clicked, I got angry and instead of backing up slowly to reduce any further damage, I stepped on the gas and went forward as hard as I could. I'll show them, my brain roared!

Stupid, stupid, stupid. In honor of preserving my foolishness, I busted the whole sideboard off my truck. And the damage cost $3,180!

What's more, when I finally stopped myself to survey the damage, I got out more heated than I ever experienced in my life. Unconsciously I locked the door and slammed it shut! Without the keys in my hand!

There I was, locked out in the cold, stranded, truck damaged, and its motor running.

About 3 hours later, my husband showed up to rescue me.

Looking Foolish Is A Powerful Influence!

I want you to get a good feel for how painful looking foolish can be. The fact is, consumers are wary for this very reason. They don't want to look foolish if they make a poor choice.

It's up to you to alleviate those types of concerns and reduce buyer's remorse in your copy.

More people take less action because they are afraid it won't be right, they are going to look dumb, or they are going to screw it up. You've got to understand your job is to acknowledge *that* reality of human nature and compensate around it.

Reassure them, direct them. Touch them. Give them room to decide without their feeling foolish.

How to Make Your Customer Feel Good

What does this mean to you? The bottom line about human nature is this: People will do more things not to participate and not buy your product because they don't want to look foolish.

They will work harder not to look foolish than they will work to gain an advantage. Accept it and factor into your strategies and your actions this reality.

Guarantee Your Customer Assurance with Triple Layered Benefits

How do you guarantee you are building your customer's confidence in your business offering? Here's how to tap into guaranteeing their feelings are taken into consideration and they feel reassured they are making the right choice.

Here's how to reduce their tendency for feeling foolish.

As you are planning your marketing materials, ask yourself these questions.

"If I were on the receiving end, why would I want this?

Why would I want to take advantage?

What's in it for me?"

Then as you are making a presentation or you're figuring out what your ad or brochure should be like. You already know to ask, "So what?" This allows you to clarify their desires and needs.

It demonstrates to people that logic and emotion by acting (buying) is so much more preferable to them than inaction (not buying), from their benefit standpoint, not yours.

Another simple way to apply this is to use a triple level benefit formula to ensure you capture the emotional triggers.

First state them a benefit of superiority over others, differentiating your product or service from all others. Let's use an electric carving knife as an example. My first level benefit statement would be: Here at last is a quiet carver. Now ask, "So what?"

Next, relate that benefit statement of <u>superiority to the customer.</u> The second level benefit statement would be: Your turkey carving noise and buzzing is gone forever. Ask again, "So what?"

Finally, tell your customer how this superiority brings an improvement to his/her life or business. The third level benefit is: For the first time, you can have a clever table conversation, or listen to your children in the background … and actually hear them.

See how that's done? This indeed is a mindset. It's all about your customers' needs and desires. See your business as interacting and enhancing people and their lives.

Using this little-known copywriting tactic will enhance how your customer gives you the attention and business you deserve! (Source: "On The Art Of Writing Copy", Herschell Gordon Lewis, 3rd Edition, 2004)

Your Action Plan:

Now it's time for your test out your own benefits to your niche market. List as many triple layered benefits that you can think of.

11. R—RESULTS: YOUR SELLING SOLUTION

All the work you've done to this point gives you the meat of the rough draft of your sales information.

Now you need to put it into an organized flowing format that includes all the relevant items you've gathered. You will now create an effective, persuasive document.

Your Action Plan

Simple? Sure... simple when you get to fill in the blanks. Take your headline, your features and benefits, and all the detail you wrote out earlier. Fill in the following template.

It holds the key to all the necessary items you need to write the best sales letter for your product, service or business concept. It includes vital information like your headers, subheads, credentials, price, guarantees, benefits and benefits and of course benefits.

Sample Letter

<"Hot Testimonial"> from a well-known person

"Here's How You Can Quickly and Easily Get
[1st Level Benefit] Guaranteed To
[2nd and 3rd Level Outcome they want]!"

Dear Friend,

How much is [product/service] worth to your business?

Suppose you could [take an easy step] and [get the compelling benefit they're looking for].

Imagine... [help them picture the ideal situation].

Now it's possible if you have the right [tools, resources, etc.].

Just look at this. 'A' is the most powerful [employee, skill, product] [you could ever hire/learn, use, etc.]. [Explain why it's so wonderful]. Simply put, [reiterate how great the benefit bullet is].

How Else Could You [1st Level Bullet] Without Sacrificing [emotional desire]?

It could take you years and can cost you a small fortune to figure out just the right combinations that make some [magic bullets] work. Until now that is.

Instead of knocking yourself out trying to come up with just the right [what they're looking for], you can now have it inside a new [product] called:

"[Name of Info Product]"

At last! Every [2nd level benefit they wanted] is here.

But don't take my word for it, here's what customers from all over the country are saying about this unique {your info category} system:

{"Testimonial"}
{"Testimonial"}
{"Testimonial"}

I know you're probably still skeptical and a bit on the conservative side but, think about this - if you keep doing the same things over and over again - you'll only succeed in getting the same results. That's why I want you to try out my proven marketing system - completely and totally risk-free! (I'll tell you about my unique guarantee in a moment.)

Which Of These Powerful Secrets
Could You Use To [3rd Level Benefit]?

[Benefit Bullet]
[Benefit Bullet]
[Benefit Bullet]
[Benefit Bullet]
[Benefit Bullet]
[Benefit Bullet]
[Benefit Bullet]
[Benefit Bullet] plus, lots more

Okay, So What's The Cost For This Incredible Resource?

Well, realize that this [whatever your product is] could easily sell for [hundreds/thousands] of dollars. In fact if you asked a top [expert] like myself, to produce [your product] for you, you'd be charged in the neighborhood of $xxxx to $xxxx, not including [some additional charge].

(I currently charge a minimum of $xxxx.xx for [job/service, etc.] . So at bare bones minimum you're getting thousands and thousands of dollars' worth of [whatever it is] at your disposal.

But I'm not going to charge you anywhere near that amount or even my minimum project price. **In fact, your total investment for [restate what they're getting] is only [$xxx.xx]**

So what's the catch? Why am I practically giving this resource away?

Well, it's really quite simple. [Explain reason why].

[#] FREE Bonuses For Ordering By Midnight [[Deadline Date]]

Free Bonus Gift #1: {Explain Bonus and give value}
Free Bonus Gift #2: {Explain Bonus and give value}
Free Bonus Gift #3: {Explain Bonus and give value}
Together these [#] free bonuses are worth more than

[double/triple, etc.] your investment in the **[Info Product Name]** -- but they're all yours absolutely free when you order by midnight [[deadline date]].

100% Risk-Free Guarantee:

Your success in using [product] is completely guaranteed. In fact, here's my 100% Better-Than-Risk-Free-Take-it-To-The-Bank Guarantee:

I personally guarantee that if you [state guarantee].

If after a full 12 months, you honestly believe I haven't delivered on this promise then let me know and I'll issue you a prompt and courteous refund. Plus, the free bonus gifts are yours to keep regardless, just for your trouble.

Is that fair or what?

That means you can try out all the [material] at my risk, while you see if they work for you or not. And if they don't produce, I honestly want you to ask for your money back. And I'll let you keep the free bonus gifts as my way of thanking you for giving [your product] a try.

There is absolutely no risk, whatsoever on your part. The burden to deliver is entirely on me.

Look at it this way -- $xxxx is really a painless drop in the bucket compared to the money you're going to waste on ineffective [whatever they're currently doing] this year. That's why...

You Really Can't Afford Not To Invest In
These [Your Product]!

It's easy to get started right away. Just [order instructions: (click here/call/fax/mail). Get ready to [big 1st Level Benefit they want].

Sincerely,

Your Name

P.S. Just think! You'll never again suffer through the pain and hassle of [big pain or hardship they're having].

(Source: Bob Bly, "Letter Writing Handbook")

CONCLUDING REMARKS

Now that you've read through this book, you know it's a lot of information and a lot of work. Please don't panic. It's time to go back and take one step at a time.

Don't be afraid to write conversationally. Don't be afraid to write everything that comes to you. The information will be cut and paste and trimmed to fit your specific needs. The information will be modified to fit your ad, a short letter, a long letter, a brochure, and any web page, blog or auto responder newsletter.

The information is what your customer needs to be convinced to buy from you. And when you "speak" to your customer in her language, she will connect with you. She will respond. You will be famous!

Your Action Plan
Bonus: 44 Ways to Please Your Customer and Maintain Fame:

1. Send direct mail – it works! And in doing so, send 2 order forms. Put them on postcards, which can be mailed back easily. You will be pleasantly surprised how this improves your results. People

lose one – and/or send one on to other business associates.
2. Offer free bonuses if they take action now – and make sure those bonuses are not sent if they order after the deadline. You must keep your word. It sends integrity energy. (You know word gets out – referral is another huge profit generating process.)
3. Offer extra incentives to past clients who are not buying from you anymore. Do what you can to get them back.
4. Offer mystery bonuses – build them up to have a very high perceived value – don't tell what it is – then surprise them with a very valuable bonus worth more than what you promised.
5. Paint pictures in the readers' minds. Reading fiction, reading highly effective copy, books on how to write picture painting stories and any literature helps stimulate imagination.
6. Tell a story – one of the best ways to pull your readers into your marketing and get them to buy. The Wall Street Journal ran a two-page story oriented sales letter talking about Two Young Men – both from the same upbringing and neighborhood - how one went on to accomplish great things and the other became his employee. This direct response ad has been running for over years and in that time it has generated well over $3 Billion in subscription sales.
7. Be sincere, educational and passionate in your writing. Do whatever it takes to get into a peak emotional state before you start writing – be it music, exercise, lots of coffee.
8. Write to a grade 7 reading level. This can be easily checked in Microsoft word – go to "Tools at top – then – Options: then Spelling and Grammar: check the box that says Show Readability Stats. Every time you do a spell check form now on it will tell

you what grade level your writing is at. This is your lowest common denominator and a guideline you must use in all your business correspondence and advertising – unless you know without a doubt that 100% of your market is at a Ph.D. level.

9. Pretend you are sitting on your couch with one of your best friends. You know that they have some possible interest in what you are selling. But they are skeptical at the best of times. What would you say to them to get them to try it out? How would you say it to them? This is exactly what your ads need to read like.

10. Be extra careful using slang. Make sure the people you are writing to use them. Golfers have their own language, tennis players, dog lovers – you name it. Each market has terms it uses that most other markets would never understand.

11. The headline is a key factor – spend 80% of your time nailing down the perfect headline. Write out dozens of headlines before you even think of narrowing down the list to the top few.

12. The first sentence is critical to keep your customer reading. Think of it this way. The goal of a headline is to get you to read the first sentence. The goal of the first sentence is to get you to read the second sentence – and so on down the path until you either place an order or call for the information promised.

13. Use letterhead as they were designed for. Put your logo at the bottom – and make it smaller. People don't care how pretty your logo is so it has no right to be at the top. The top of your ad and letters should always be reserved for headlines. Also, the place where you usually put their name and address at the top – get rid of it – they know their name and where they work. Personalize the salutation. At the top the only thing you need is a headline and appropriate subheads.

On websites, use a quality header! The header is the graphic at the top of your site. A mistake a lot of people make is putting a headline in the header graphic and expecting results. Your header needs to look professional, have a title and tagline, but keep headlines in the pages themselves.

And example of a title and tagline would be "WordPress Website Writer". The tagline would be "How to Set Up Real Websites and Blogs in WordPress Fast and Painless" Guess who!

14. If you have an exceptionally powerful offer – summarize it right up front – your first paragraph on each of your pages or promotional pieces should be a summary of what it is that you are writing about.
15. Use the word **'You'** as much as humanly possible. And that means in your Abut me or About Us pages on your website as well. How can you do this? Not only are you telling people who you are, what you do, tell them why you're relevant to their lives! Then you can talk to them about them – "YOU"!
16. The word 'free' still carries enormous weight – despite its overuse today. Make your 'free' offer incredibly valuable.
17. Always use a **PS!** The average reader looks at the headline first, then if interested goes right to the end to see who wrote this and will read the PS. If you maintain their interest, they will go back to the start and read from there. This works brilliantly in blog posts as well as newsletters and pages!
18. Use pictures of people using your products – never just the product if possible. AND – always put a caption under the photograph. Wordpress websites make this simple and easy to do.
19. In fact, let me mention about Wordpress. You're making a huge mistake in today's mobile-friendly

and online community if you don't create your website in WordPress. WordPress is the ultimate content management system for both a blog and a website. It's instantly upgradable with literally thousands of free plugins. In fact, the top dozen or so are listed at the end of this section. What's more, unless you purchase a specific template, WordPress is free! And no, not those premade website solutions like wordpress.com or Blogspot – but http://www.wordpress.org

20. Of course, if you want support to set it up and create copy, or you have a website and don't quite know how to have it work for you generating subscribers, then you need to check out my special offers here. http://patriciaogilvie.com/about-wordpress-websites

    When you decide which package suits your needs, I will personally teach you how to set it up, how to run it, how to maintain it, and how to do all the marketing copy good stuff to begin collecting subscribers and make profits!

21. Talk **benefits, benefits, and more benefits**! What is in it for them? Only the true techy cares if it has 45 GB of disk space and 256MB of ram. Buyers care that there is enough disk space to store all their files, letters, and photographs for the next 7 years – and there is enough memory to run their kids' favorite graphics game.

22. Tie in your copy with newsworthy topics, events happening, local interests, and personal interests' stories. Blogs are so powerful. And then broadcast that information through your social media applications.

23. If your product is not sold in stores – tell them! This gives it exclusivity and makes it more likely that they will want to order if they know they cannot get it anywhere else.

24. If you can, delay their payments. "Pay nothing now" is a very powerful promise that has built many multi-million dollar businesses. Or, if some money is required – offer them a payment plan over the next 6 or 12 months. People may scoff at paying $1,295 out of their pocket today but those same people may be very willing to pay $110 per month for 12 months – even if it means they pay a much higher rate. E-commerce has never been quicker or simpler to install.
25. Get them involved in your letter or ad through questions, surveys, and check boxes – whatever you can do to keep them interested.
26. Talk about some product negatives. No product or service in the world is perfect – be honest with them about that and you will be the only honest person they have come across in business.
27. Tell them the limitations, or the catch, or the one thing that you can never use it for. Incredibly powerful when you are the one to bring this up – they are already thinking, "what's the catch" so tell them what it is.
28. Write the ad copy so that when they order, they can easily explain it to their spouse and friends why this is such an incredible deal.
29. Test this out – write the letter as if it is coming from your spouse to them. Pretend that you didn't know about it and your spouse did this behind your back. Sign it in their name. Explain why it is from them – what they are doing – why they are doing it that way.
30. When you have written your letter or ad – put it aside for a day or two. Then come back to it and read it again. Still strong? Many times this break will show you areas that you totally missed the previous times you read it.
31. Offer your customers a variety of e-commerce

options, credit cards, Paypal, ClickBank to help ease their buying process.
32. Test sending it to a company without a person's name. Or send it to a certain level of personnel (Manager of Human Resources). This can get it many more hands this way and you just may find it performs better than addressing it specifically to a person.
33. Always test your new ads and letters to your existing client base. Test a small group first – see what results you get. Then test larger groups of your clients. If it does not convince them – it will not convince people that have never heard of you before.
34. Send newspaper articles and magazines articles of your company to prospects to increase believability. Seed your customers. If you don't collect mailing addresses, you won't benefit from this awesome marketing tactic. However, frankly, people are looking and buying using smart phones more and more! I wasn't sure if I should have created a new Chapter for this topic, however, I will give you a synopsis here.
35. Smartphones are it! Mobility directs traffic to your website, social media and all your advertising and marketing material. That means your website also needs to look good on the computer, on an ipad, and in the small palm of your customers hand!
What you need is WordPress that is responsive. Write that down – responsive. This means, it morphs to look good on pretty much any device.
You can get some unmodified versions free from http://www.wordpress.org/themes/responsive
36. When they first order - send out an immediate thank you letter that day reaffirming their decision to purchase. Then send out your product a day or two later. I registered for a program recently and a

few weeks later received a thank you card in the mail. Felt good!
37. Test window style envelopes so they can peek into instead of plain white unmarked envelopes. Then test white envelopes with teaser headlines on the outside. You never know which one your market will respond best to – until you test it.
38. Put a very unusual message on the outside of the envelope.
39. Personalize the headline on the outside of the envelope.
40. Include a reply envelope – test one that is stamped and not stamped.
41. Always use real postage stamps on your envelopes – never metered mail. Make it look as personalized as possible – not like it came straight from a machine. Order stamps with your own picture on it!
42. Always remember that the majority of sales are not made on the first contact. Follow up with a series of letters, postcards, and incentives with all of your leads and inquiries.
43. First time clients should receive an extra special thank you note.
44. Send letters quarterly just to say thanks for being a customer – include your latest marketing materials in the envelope – but don't ask for an order on this type of mailer – this is just a note to say thanks.

Congratulations!

By reading and hopefully completing the action plans in this book you are now ready to serve your customer again and again. You've hooked them and they're pleased to become your repeat customer!

You now know how to apply these fame factors: practical strategies for creating your customer commitment.

THE FAME FACTORS

You're famous! The trick is to apply these principles in hard copy and especially online where everybody lives today!

ABOUT THE AUTHOR

Say hello to Patricia Ogilvie, your Direct Response Freelance Copywriter & Proofreader. Her experience and qualifications include the following:
Trained in Advanced Level Direct Response Copy Writing - American Writers and Artists Institute; Former **Systems Analyst** known for intense research, analysis and attention to detail; and in multiple projects.

Stays current on new advertising trends for different products and services; **Thorough** understanding of Direct Response formula – proven record of writing winning controls; And National Member, Canadian Association of Professional Speakers.

Patricia is married to Randy and lives at Alberta Beach, near Edmonton, Alberta. Edmonton is the city boasting the world's largest Shopping Mall in the only debt-free province in Canada. Ironic analogy, isn't it?

She's been a professional copywriter, editor and speaker for over 15 years, and has written fiction, non-fiction, poetry, numerous e-books as well as distance learning courses, multimedia CD's and scripts.

She is the author of 14 books, several of which are best sellers and all available on Amazon.

Your Action Plan

Contact me at
https://auntisays.com/project/about-me/ and tell me that you want written, edited or proofread

MORE BOOKS BY PATRICIA OGILVIE

I f you like this book, you'll love the 1st, 2nd, 3rd, and 4th inspirational adult coloring books in my series of stress reducer and fun increasers.

Look for Bag lady, Marbles, and Radical Self-Respect, and the public favorite, Life Lessons for women on my website, auntisays.com.

Plus, there are more books available:

Amazon Best Seller: Wild Mind: Remembering Last Week's Notes Today 2017

The Most Powerful Person on Earth 2017

Believe in Magic 2016

Good Better Best 2016 Children's book

How to Keep the Ground from Shaking 2017

How to Be the BOSS of Your Own Money 2017

Find all these at www.auntisays.com/shop

And please do leave a comment on Amazon for me. I would love to hear your experience and how you've found releasing the fear of what others think.

Appreciate you!

Patricia

www.ingramcontent.com/pod-product-compliance
Lightning Source LLC
Chambersburg PA
CBHW071412220526
45469CB00004B/1261